The Prophecy of

MAGOG

and ISRAEL

Ezekiel 38–39

Is the U.S. in Prophecy?

Michael Pearl

International bestselling author of

GOOD & EVIL: THE ULTIMATE COMIC BOOK BIBLE

Publication date: January 2016

1st Printing: 5,000 - January 2016
2nd Printing: 5,000 - January 2021

Print ISBN: 978-1-61644-083-1
ePub ISBN: 978-1-61644-084-8
ePDF ISBN: 978-1-61644-085-5

All Scripture quotations are taken from the King James Holy Bible

Library of Congress Control Number: 2015920271

This publication is designed to provide accurate and authoritative information in regard to the subject matter covered. It is sold with the understanding that the author or the publisher is not engaged in rendering any type of professional services. If expert assistance is required, the services of a competent professional should be sought.

1. Bible Prophecy 2. End Times 3. Ezekiel 4. Scripture
5. United States 6. Israel 7. Gog 8. Magog
I. Pearl, Michael II. The Prophecy of Magog and Israel: Ezekiel 38–39

The Prophecy of Magog and Israel: Ezekiel 38–39 may be purchased at special quantity discounts for churches, donor programs, fund raising, book clubs, or educational purposes for churches, congregations, schools and universities. Rights and Licensing in other languages and international sales opportunities are available. For more information contact:

No Greater Joy
1000 Pearl Road
Pleasantville TN 37033
(866) 292-9936
ngj@nogreaterjoy.org

Cover design by Megan Van Vuren and Aaron Aprile
Interior layout by Michael Pearl and Aaron Aprile

Publisher: No Greater Joy Ministries, Inc.
www.nogreaterjoy.org

Printed in the United States of America

Foreword

There is no cause to speculate about the coming apocalypse. The Bible is quite clear on the subject. There will be an attempted invasion of Israel by a conglomerate of world powers, primarily Japhetic. That includes all of Europe, Russia, and the United States, along with Canada, Australia and more. The UN fits the bill.

All my life I have heard Bible teachers say that the invading force of Magog is Russian, as seen in the names Meshech and Tubal, which we were told were former spellings of Moscow and Tobolsk. It turns out that there is no basis for such an assertion. To the contrary, the invading force is composed of descendants of Magog, the grandson of Noah, assisted by Iran, Turkey, Libya, and Ethiopia.

The invasion will fail because God is back in the business of preserving Israel for its coming King.

Read all about it.

—Michael Pearl

Table of Contents

"I am the LORD: that is my name:
and my glory will I not give to another, neither my praise
to graven images. Behold, the former things are come to pass,
and **new things do I declare: before they spring forth
I tell you of them.**"

(Isaiah 42:8–9)

"I have **declared the former things from the beginning;**
and they went forth out of my mouth, and I shewed them;
I did them suddenly, and **they came to pass.**

"I have even from the beginning declared it to thee;
before it came to pass I shewed it thee: lest thou shouldest
say, Mine idol hath done them, and my graven image,
and my molten image, hath commanded them."

(Isaiah 48:3, 5)

"Remember the former things of old: for I am God,
and there is none else; I am God, and there is none like me,
**Declaring the end from the beginning, and from
ancient times the things that are not yet done,** saying,
My counsel shall stand, and I will do all my pleasure."

(Isaiah 46:9–10)

"Let all the nations be gathered together,
and let the people be assembled: who among them
can declare this, and shew us former things? let them
bring forth their witnesses, that they may be justified:
or **let them hear, and say, It is truth.**"

(Isaiah 43:9)

Ras e... Haifa 'Nasa

En-Nas

'Affule

Atlit

Tantura   Leddjun

Djenin
114

Qaisariye
(Caesarea)

Tubas

Nahr Iskanderune   El   Nabulu

Mukhalid

ISRAEL   Qalqiliye   Selfit

Tel Aviv   Sahl Sarou   Djel-As

Yafa   103

(Jaffa)
Lydda   Ramallah   Jeriko

Lidd

Er-Ramle   EL-QUDS-ESH-SH
Yebna   790   JERI

Esdud   Beit Djala   Betlehe

El-Medjdel   Sahl Sefela   Beit Djibrin
Hebron (El-Kha
927

Ghaza   Wadi el-Hesi

Wadi Ghaza   W. esh-Sheri'a   W. es-Sey

Edh-Dhaheriye   El-Kusife

Tell Refah
Bir es-Seba

Rafah   240
eina   adi es-Siny

Sheikh Suweid

Arish   Biyar el-Asludj   Wadi

Ezekiel 38–39

Watching Prophecy Being Fulfilled

There is an end-time prophecy in Ezekiel 38–39 that has fascinated me since I first started studying the Bible fifty-five years ago. Gog, along with Meshech and Tubal and several nations including Persia (Iran), Ethiopia, and Libya attempt to invade Israel and are supernaturally destroyed by God so that he "will be known in the eyes of many nations, and they shall know that I am the LORD" (Ezekiel 38:23).

In the past few months, conditions have rapidly aligned with the potential fulfillment of this 2,700-year-old prophecy. Fulfillment seems imminent. Our redemption draws nearer with every newscast.

During the twentieth century and up until the present, evangelical prophecy teachers have held to the belief that the invading force is Russia. I, too, have repeated that standard line, not having done any original research. It is not the first time I have been wrong due to accepting conventional opinion garnered from people I respect—and continue to respect. It is very time-consuming to study every belief we inherit—probably impossible. After independent study, my conclusion is that Russia may well be a part of the commanding force of Magog, but so is the United States of America, along with the rest of the Western Japhetic nations, as well as some Middle Eastern Japhetic nations like Turkey and Iran.

There are three approaches to identifying the invading forces:

1. Bible chronology
2. Historical records
3. Genetics (a recent resource)

The most weight must be given to the Bible itself because not only is it perfect in its historical references but it is also the most thorough and cohesive document on the subject of the origin of ancient peoples. But as in all truth, we will expect to see history and genetics supporting our Biblical interpretation. Accurate Bible interpretation

> **Accurate Bible interpretation and true science are never in conflict.**

and true science are never in conflict. If there is a conflict, it is because one or both have misrepresented the evidence.

The Prophecy

In Ezekiel chapters 38 and 39, the prophet records the very words God spoke to him. In the **"latter years,"** Israel will be attacked from the north through Togarmah (Turkey) by a large federation of nations under the headship of Magog (Caucasian descendants of Japheth) who dwell in the "north parts." Magog, Meshech, and Tubal will be assisted by "a great company, and a might army" of "many people" from the north with three additional countries: Persia from the east (Iran), and two countries from the south: Ethiopia and Libya.

Magog, Meshech, and Tubal are not the names of countries, but of ethnic groups, the descendants of Japheth through his son Magog (Genesis 10:2). After Noah's flood, Japheth's sons begin a northwesterly migration, eventually spreading out to occupy all of Europe, Russia, Ukraine, Poland, the Slavic states, Great Britain, and eventually the United States, Australia, Canada, New Zealand, etc.

Some American Christians have developed a tradition of saying that Magog is Russia, no doubt encouraged by ethnocentrisms. It is easy for the Western free world to believe that the "Evil Empire" will invade Israel, but the idea that Europe and the U.S. might be the instigators of this invasion has been unthinkable. But it is much more thinkable now than it was seven years ago.

Modern writers think Magog is Russia because of the similarity of the words Meshech to Moscow, and Tubal to Tobolsk, but Russia didn't exist at the time of the prophecy. However, according to numerous historical records, including Josephus of the first century and many ancient rabbis, the descendants of Magog did exist in the area north of Turkey, below the Black Sea, and across southern Europe. The earliest Russia began to form would have been around 800 AD,

1,500 years after the prophecy. Moscow came into existence around 1147 AD, and the Russian Empire was founded in 1721. The ancient names for Moscow and Tobolsk were *Slavi* and *Wends*, not Meshech and Tubal. There is nothing in history that links Meshech and Tubal with these two Russian cities. It is just a matter of the words sharing some consonants.

> The ancient names for Moscow and Tobolsk were ***Slavi*** and ***Wends***, not Meshech and Tubal.

And if one *could* find hard evidence that Meshech and Tubal are in Russia, that would exclude Russia from being the primary mover—Magog. For Magog is said to be the "chief prince" of Meshech and Tubal, indicating a difference in political structure. The head prince indicates one that leads a coalition of powers while not being the actual ruler of either of them. This fits the concept of a UN-led "peacekeeping force" under Western leadership. Turkey is the land from which Israel will be attacked, as clearly stated by the geographic description given by the prophet, yet the leader, Magog, will be "prince" over a large number of different nations.

Magog Is Worldwide

In Revelation 20:8 we learn that "Gog and Magog" is a universal combination of nations, "which are in the **four quarters of the earth,** Gog and Magog, to gather them together to battle: the number of whom is as the sand of the sea." Even after the millennial reign of Christ over the nations, the worldwide descendants of Magog will still maintain their ethnic identification. **<u>The fact that Scripture places Magog in the four quarters of the earth would eliminate any single nation from exclusively holding that designation.</u>** History and genetic studies support the worldwide distribution of Magog's descendants.

It is also noteworthy that whereas the prophet named the countries of Persia and Libya, he did not name a particular country as the driving force from the north; rather, he goes all the way back to the table of nations in Genesis 10, immediately after the flood, and references the Japhetic line as opposed to the Hamitic and Semitic.

Genetics place the origin of Russians in the Slavic peoples, Poland, and Eastern Europe. So for that reason, not the similarity of names, Russia may be a significant part of the invading force, having descended from Japheth as did Europe, Great Britain, and the United States.

Amazing Prophetic Accuracy

It is fascinating that of the more than one hundred people groups and nations in the seventh century BC within reach of Israel, the three that the prophet names still exist today and are aligned against Israel. The people of Ezekiel's day would never suspect Libya and Ethiopia of posing a threat to Israel. If the prophet had named the more obvious Tyre, Philistia, Edom, the Amorites, or any of the Canaanite nations that were a constant threat, the prophecy would have been believable in Ezekiel's day, but in time it would have been proven false, for all those people groups no longer exist upon the earth. Not only are the nations gone, but the ethnic lineage has disappeared. The only way to explain the incredible fact that Ezekiel was able to see 2,700 years into the future and accurately predict the surviving nations that would be enemies of Israel is by the omniscient and omnipotent God. That is no small prophecy.

Japhetic Nations

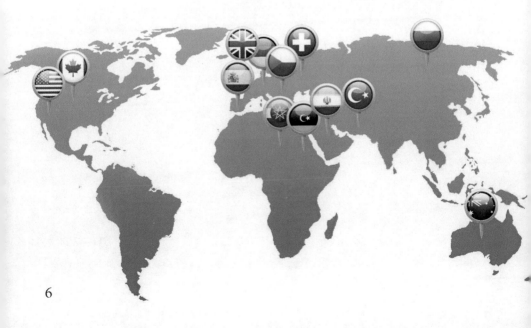

The Prophecy Is Also Extraordinary in the Way It Describes Israel

The prophet dates it as "in the latter years" and says Israel is "the land that is brought back from the sword [war], and is gathered out of many people [nations where they were dispersed], . . . which have been always waste [the land was waste before the Jews occupied it]:

but it is brought forth out of the nations [United Nations], and they shall dwell safely all of them" (Ezekiel 38:8). There are six specific details in the prophecy. How could the prophet know 2,700 years beforehand that Israel would be "brought forth out of the [United] nations"?

In 1947 the United Nations General Assembly allotted the Jews a place in their ancient homeland. That is a perfect description of historical events. They were "brought forth out of the nations" as boatload after boatload were dumped on the shores of their embattled, ancient homeland. Many were immediately put into battle carrying sticks. This extraordinary event occurred during my lifetime and the Scripture dates it as "the latter years." I have lived my entire life knowing I am living in the last days before the coming of Christ.

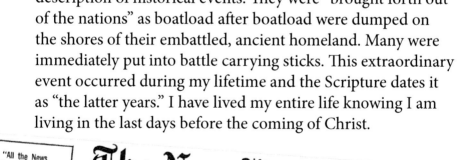

Wrong on Salvation—Wrong on Prophecy

In 1946 a Church of Christ (Campbellite) preacher wrote a book disparaging the idea of a pre-Tribulation rapture and a literal millennial reign of Christ upon the earth. His primary argument was that for premillennialism to be true, the Jews would have to occupy their ancient land of Israel, and it was obvious to him that such a thing could never happen. At the

time of his writing, two-thirds of the Jews living in Europe (about half of their worldwide number) had been killed in the Holocaust. Furthermore, Britain occupied Palestine, favoring the Arabs. Israel had been dispersed throughout the nations for 1,866 years. Survivors of the Holocaust were pitiful physical wrecks. It appeared their end had come, not their redemption. But within a year of the publication of his book, Israel was a nation of Jews who had driven the English out (King David Hotel) and defeated their enemies in battle. The Star of David flew over their ancient homeland and God was worshipped

in ancient Hebrew, the language in which the Scriptures were originally written. Needless to say, the publisher had a lot of books sent to the dump. Never doubt your Bible, no matter how far-fetched it seems.

On the shores of the Danube, one can see 60 pairs of shoes of all sizes lining the shore. During the years of 1944–1945, Jews were forced to remove their shoes before facing a firing squad of Arrow Cross militiamen at short range. Their bodies fell into the Danube, and were carried away by the current. Today, the shoes (which were cast out of iron and are now rusting) continue to line the shores of the Danube in memorial to the Jews that lost their lives.

Other Invading Forces

GOMER

Ezekiel 38:6 names two more descendants of Japheth (Caucasians/white/Aryan) that participate in the invasion of Israel, Gomer and Togarmah (Genesis 10:3). There is no objection to the fact that Gomer refers mainly to Celtic peoples, including Gauls, Britons, and Irish, which now represent not only the Western European nations but also the United States. By the fourth century BC, they spread over much of what is now France, Belgium, Switzerland,

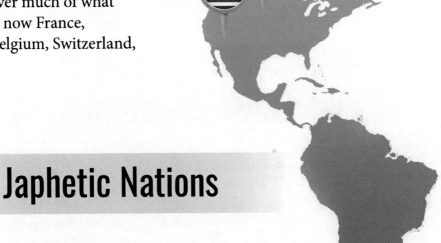

Japhetic Nations

Southern Germany, Austria and the Czech Republic, and southern Russia.

You will notice an overlap of the people groups and geographical locations by the different factions, all descendants of Japheth, because the family consistently migrated north and west, mingling as they competed for territory and conquering one another from time to time.

The history of Russia, Europe, and Great Britain is the history of the sons of Japheth struggling for territory and supremacy.

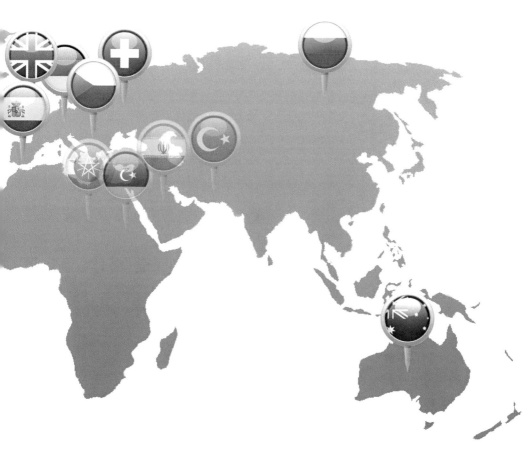

TOGARMAH

The prophet includes in the invasion force "the house of Togarmah of the north quarters, and all his bands: and many people with thee" (Ezekiel 38:6). Ancient Jewish sources list Togarmah as the father of the Turkic peoples. This fits the text's geographic reference of the people north of Israel.

Today there are 170 million people speaking a Turkic language. At present, there are six independent Turkic countries: Azerbaijan, Kazakhstan, Kyrgyzstan, Turkmenistan, Turkey, and Uzbekistan. The Turkic lineage is also Japhetic (white, non-Arab, non-Semitic, non-Hamitic). The reason the prophet singles it out from Magog and Gomer is most likely due to the fact that though it is Japhetic, it is Muslim and is set apart from the Western world by its culture and religion.

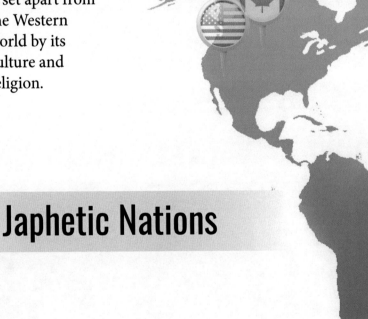

Japhetic Nations

The invasion comes down through Turkey with "all his bands: and many people." So we can expect all the Turkic "-stan" countries to be in league with Turkey and Magog.

PERSIA

The Persians (Iranians), in contrast with the rest of the Arabic Muslims, are also Aryan/descendants of Japheth. In fact the term Aryan comes from the word Iranian.

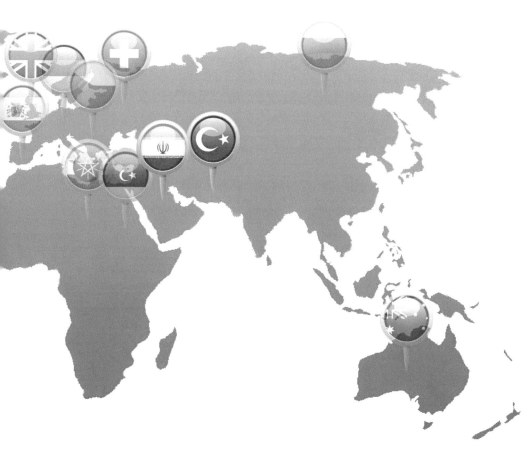

ETHIOPIA

(Hebrew: Cush, Son of Ham, father of Nimrod, Gen 10:6–8.)

Ethiopia was the land occupied by the descendants of Cush and located around the southern parts of the Nile. The Ethiopia of Ezekiel's day encompassed most of Northern Africa with the exception of Egypt. These are the only Hamites (black race) to assist in the invasion, but they will come down from the north through Turkey as well.

This alignment looks an awful lot like a United Nations operation headed by Western powers commanding some of the nations surrounding Israel.

LIBYA

A nation of Northern Africa, origin of name unknown, Libya is 90% Arab. As a nation, not necessarily a people group, it will assist in the invasion of Israel from the north, down through Turkey.

Apparently the countries from the south will be transported to Turkey, which will be a staging area for the assault.

Other Nations

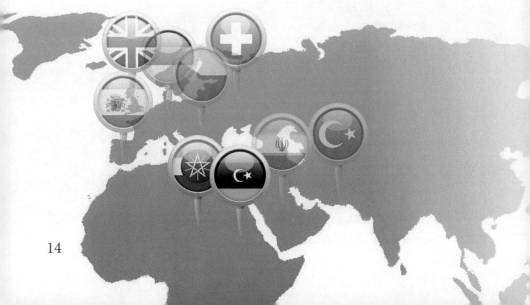

Meshech (Genesis 10:2), son of Japheth, who traded with Israel in 593 BC, is mentioned with Tubal, plus "all her multitude" (Ezekiel 32:26), as if the two are the heads of a large number of various peoples.

Javan, Tubal, and Meshech, they were thy merchants: they traded the persons of men and vessels of brass in thy market. (Ezekiel 27:13)

Tubal (Genesis 10:2), son of Japheth. According to Isaiah 66:19, Tubal is among the isles that are "afar off." Tubal, it seems, are the people of the Asiatic highland west of the Upper Euphrates, the southern range of the Caucasus on the east side of the Black Sea. Meshech and Tubal, frequently mentioned together, are part of the ancestors of Russia, Europe, and Britain and the Americas.

Prophetic History of Shem, Ham, and Japheth

The history of nations was predicted by Noah 4,338 years ago, after the flood. "God shall enlarge Japheth, and he shall dwell in the tents of Shem; and Canaan shall be his servant" (Genesis 9:27). We have seen that the history of Japheth has been one of enlargement, advancing into the wilderness of Asia all the way to the Arctic Circle (Russia), continuing west to all of Europe, Britain, and the Americas, then on to Australia, New Zealand, and the Pacific Islands. The descendants of Shem have dwelt in the same region throughout history. The Chinese, Japanese, and Jews have not conquered the world and created empires on which the sun never sets, as have the descendants of Japheth.

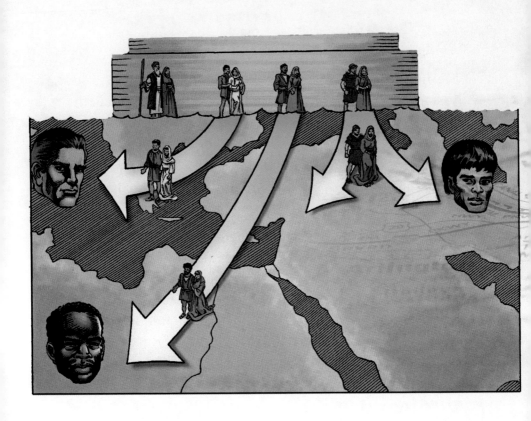

But God has dwelt in the tents of Shem. All of the seven major religions began with Shem. Jews are from Shem. God dwelt in a temple erected by descendants of Shem. The church was founded on Jesus and his twelve apostles, all from Shem. The first several thousand converts to Christianity were from Shem, and the Bible was written by Shem's descendants.

Then the prophecy says "Canaan shall be his *[Shem's]* servant." That is not the Hamitic race as a whole, just one of the descendants of Ham (Genesis 10:6). In accordance with Noah's prophecy, Shem (the Jews) conquered the land of Canaan and made servants of them until their eventual total demise.

Again, how miraculous that Noah could anticipate the history of his three sons!

Summary of Magog

This northern federation of Magog, Meshech, Tubal, and Gomer encompasses:

- **British Isles**
  Celtic, Gauls, Irish, Welsh, Britons (Gomer)

- **Scots**
  Magog, according to the Milesian genealogy

- **Anglo-Saxons**
  Gomer, Magog, and Meshech

- **France**
  Gaul, Britons (Gomer); Franks, Goths, other Germanic peoples (Gomer, Magog, and Meshech); Gascons (Tubal)

- **Spain**
  Celtiberians (Gomer and Tubal)

- **Basques**
  (Tubal)

- **Goths**
  (Meshech)

- **United States**
  Every one of the above mentioned, though the leadership is from British/Irish stock (Gomer, Magog)

Exceptions to the Invading Force: Sheba and Dedan

> **Sheba, and Dedan, and the merchants of Tarshish,** with all the young lions thereof, shall say unto thee, Art thou come to take a spoil? hast thou gathered thy company to take a prey? to carry away silver and gold, to take away cattle and goods, to take a great spoil? **(Ezekiel 38:13)**

Ezekiel's prophecy names exceptions to the invading force. Sheba and Dedan were great-grandsons of Ham. Solomon received the queen of Sheba from the south. History well documents that Sheba was in southwestern Arabia, presently Saudi Arabia and Yemen, as was Dedan, a station on the caravan road between Tema and Medina.

> The burden upon Arabia. In the forest in Arabia shall ye lodge, O ye travelling companies of Dedanim. **(Isaiah 21:13)**

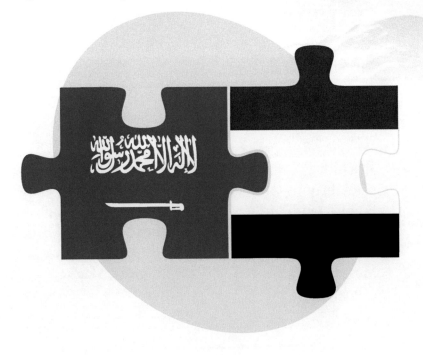

Saudi Arabia and Yemen are not part of the attacking coalition. They stand afar and ask the question, "Why have you invaded Israel; are you come to take a spoil?" Perhaps their proximity will give them reason for concern.

Ships of Tarshish

The annals of the Assyrian king Esarhaddon (681–669 BC) place Tarshish on the southern Spanish coast by the Strait of Gibraltar. Ten times the Scriptures speak of the "ships of Tarshish" and of the trade Israel did with them.

Merchants from Spain will be troubled by the invasion because it cuts into their trade, which will cause them to question the motive of Magog and his great number of accomplices.

History in Advance

You can read Ezekiel 38–39 to see the drama unfolding. Space allows only a brief overview of events.

In the "latter days" a large force of many nations will come "like a cloud to cover the land" (Ezekiel 38:9). Their original purpose for forming the military coalition is for reasons other than an invasion of Israel. They are there to exert needed force in a troubled region, but at the same time, while they

are in the vicinity, "shall things come into thy *[Magog and forces]* mind, and thou shalt think an evil thought: And thou shalt say, I will go up to the land of unwalled villages *[Israel]*; I will go to them that are at rest, that dwell safely, all of them dwelling without walls, and having neither bars nor gates, To take a spoil, and to take a prey; to turn thine hand upon the desolate places *that are now* inhabited, and upon the people *that are* gathered out of the nations, which have gotten cattle and goods, that dwell in the midst of the land" (38:10–12).

What the invading force does not realize is that God has seduced them into taking this action against his people Israel. For God says, "I will bring thee against my land, that the heathen may know me, when I shall be sanctified in thee, O Gog, before their eyes" (38:16). God brings them against Israel so he can destroy their invading forces in such a manner that everyone knows God did it, thus glorifying himself.

Verses 19–22 speak of events that match conditions in the Tribulation. But it is clear that this invasion is not the Battle of Armageddon. This is a different event that precedes Armageddon and, I think, leads to the introduction of Antichrist. I do think there is a very good chance that this event takes place before the rapture of the church, although I cannot be certain. If it does take place in the Great Tribulation, it will precede Armageddon.

Worldwide Judgment

God warns:

> I will send a fire on Magog, and among them that dwell carelessly in the isles. **(39:6)**

> And they that dwell in the cities of Israel shall go forth, and shall set on fire and burn the weapons, both the shields and the bucklers, the bows and the arrows, and the handstaves, and the spears, and they shall burn them with fire **seven years:** So that they shall take no wood out of the field, neither cut down *any* out of the forests; for they shall burn the weapons with fire: and they shall spoil those that spoiled them, and rob those that robbed them, saith the Lord GOD. And it shall come to pass in that day, *that* I will give unto Gog a place there of graves in Israel, the valley of the passengers **on the east of the sea** *[east of the Dead Sea]*: and it shall stop the *noses* of the passengers: and there shall they bury Gog and all his multitude: and they shall call *it* The **valley of Hamon-gog. (39:9–11)**

God will destroy five-sixths (39:2) of the invading forces by means of a fire from heaven (38:22). We know it will not be nuclear because the world will recognize it to be the work of God.

There will be so many dead that it says the stench "shall stop the noses of the passengers" (39:11).

For seven months following the destruction the entire nation is engaged in burying Magog's dead. At the end of seven months Israel hires men to work full-time in the job of burying the dead and cleansing the land (39:12–15). An entire city will be built to manage the employees who are cleansing the land (39:16).

There is one teaser in the passage that lends credence to the possibility that this event begins before the rapture of the church. After the cleansing of the land, Israel will gather the leftover weaponry and supplies of the enemy and burn them for fuel for **seven years** (39:9). It seems that the seven years follows the seven months of all Israel engaged in burying the dead. The entire period in which the Tribulation occurs is just seven years, preceded by the Rapture and followed by the second coming and Millennium. So either the destruction takes place at least seven months before the Rapture, or the burning of implements continues into the Millennium. It's a thought. We don't have to know for sure because we will have a ringside seat and can ride our white horse through the area when we return to the earth with our Lord, the Captain of our salvation.

The United States in Prophecy

American Christians have maintained an insatiable curiosity to discover the U.S. in prophecy. "Do we survive until the end? Are we destroyed by nuclear weapons before the Rapture? Do we have any part in the great battle of Armageddon?" The U.S. most certainly is in prophecy, but not as one might wish.

People unfamiliar with the Bible reason that since the Bible does indeed contain a great many prophecies of nations and end-time events, it would certainly include a nation as influential and powerful as the U.S. There is vanity in expecting to be important enough to be included.

A fundamental misunderstanding persists as to the nature of Bible prophecy. Yes, God very specifically predicts the future of many nations and events. But God is not into show business. He has not attempted to convince the world of his omniscience through prophecy—predicting tantalizing details to stimulate our faith and provide us with ongoing proof of his existence. Nor is he concerned that each nation know the details of their future.

> **God is not into show business.**

Those familiar with the whole Bible know that all end-time prophecy is in regard to Israel. The coming Tribulation is called "Jacob's trouble" (Jeremiah 30:7). You remember Jacob, the father of the twelve tribes of Israel. That end-time battle is also called "the day of Jezreel" (Hosea 1:11), named after the valley in northern Israel where the battle of Armageddon takes place. God spoke to Daniel about the end of the age, saying, "Seventy weeks are determined upon thy people [Israel] and upon thy holy city, to finish the transgression, and to make an end of sins, and to make reconciliation for iniquity, and to bring in everlasting righteousness, and to seal up the vision and prophecy, and to anoint the most Holy" (Daniel 9:24). That seven-year period is solely in regard to events in Israel.

> When nations have blessed Israel, they have been blessed. When nations have cursed Israel, they have been cursed.

Remember our prophecy in Ezekiel 38–39 that named all the people groups and nations? The events were mentioned only as they related to Israel. Bible history and world history are the account of God fulfilling his promises to Abraham.

> And I will make of thee a great nation, and I will bless thee, and make thy name great; and thou shalt be a blessing: And I will bless them that bless thee, and curse him that curseth thee: and in thee shall all families of the earth be blessed. **(Genesis 12:2–3)**

When nations have blessed Israel, they have been blessed. When nations have cursed Israel, they have been cursed. As long as the United States of America blessed God's people, God blessed us, but we are seeing a definite shift away from support of Israel. Anti-Semitism is on the rise worldwide, as well as here at home. Also, much of prophecy is delivered by the prophets as a warning to Israel (Leviticus 26:14–22). Sometimes the prophet spoke judgment on nations that were enemies of Israel, as he did with Tyre (Ezekiel 26) and scores of other nations.

Even many of the churches are becoming anti-Jewish. The most blatant form of discrimination against Israel is what could be accurately described as "displacement theology," held by the Roman Catholic Church, the Orthodox Church, and the Calvinists—the idea that the church has displaced Israel and that God will no longer fulfill his earthly promises to Jacob's seed. Judgment will fall on the U.S. because of our failure to fully support the nation of Israel. Like it or not, God is definitely ethnocentric.

> **Like it or not, God is definitely ethnocentric.**

> Behold, the nations are as a drop of a bucket, and are counted as the small dust of the balance: behold, he taketh up the isles as a very little thing. All nations before him are as nothing; and they are counted to him less than nothing, and vanity. (**Isaiah 40:15, 17**)

Who Is The Antichrist?

One of the most misunderstood doctrines of Scripture concerns antichrist, due mainly to the many popular books and movies on the subject. If one were to write an accurate novel that covered the tribulation period, it would not be a pleasant read. There would be no love stories, no second chances, no one getting "born again," no heroes fighting the antichrist system and surviving.

In reality, the many Christian books and movies have actually prepared the way for antichrist to deceive the world into thinking that he is the Christ. The biblical facts concerning antichrist are far different from popular belief. This little book will point you in the right direction and launch your study of this critical subject.

Written by Michael Pearl. 96 pages.

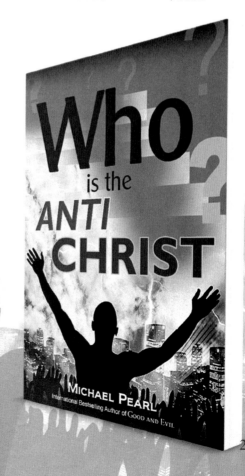

Parted the Land

The United States of America, along with the Magog-funded and -led United Nations, has "parted" God's land.

When a U.S. citizen is born in Jerusalem, Israel, our federal government will not permit passports to state Jerusalem, Israel, as the place of birth, for that would be recognizing Jerusalem as part of Israel. Every president since Israel was formed has promoted the parting of God's land. Read what God thinks about it in the following verse:

> I will also gather all nations, and will bring them down into the valley of Jehoshaphat [*Armageddon*], and will plead with them there for my people and for my heritage Israel, whom they have scattered among the nations, and **parted my land. (Joel 3:2)**

> For thus saith the LORD of hosts; After the glory hath he sent me unto the nations which spoiled you: **for he that toucheth you toucheth the apple of his eye. (Zechariah 2:8)**

The United States of America

I have said the United States is definitely in prophecy. So where?

We established that Gog and Magog are the Gentile nations scattered throughout the world. Look at Revelation 20:8 again. "And shall go out to deceive the nations which are in the **four quarters of the earth, Gog and Magog,** to gather them together to battle: the number of whom is as the sand of the sea." The citizens of the U.S. are mostly descendants of Japheth. That makes us part of Magog. So when Ezekiel quotes God as saying, "And I will send a fire on Magog, and among them that **dwell carelessly in the isles:** and they shall know that I am the LORD" (Ezekiel 39:6), we know that includes the U.S.

The text says that as Magog attacks Israel, the citizens of Magog will be dwelling "carelessly in the isles." The Jews referred to places accessed by sea as "isles." Cyprus, Spain, Britain, or the United States (and many more) would be classified as isles.

The prophecy, then, is that the United States, along with other Japhetic nations "which are in the four quarters of the earth" will be set on fire. And that is not a reference to burning tires in the streets of Baltimore and Los Angeles.

2 Peter 3:9–13

9 The Lord is not slack concerning his promise, as some men count slackness; but is longsuffering to us-ward, not willing that any should perish, but that all should come to repentance.

10 But the day of the Lord will come as a thief in the night; in the which the heavens shall pass away with a great noise, and the elements shall melt with fervent heat, **the earth also and the works that are therein shall be burned up.**

11 Seeing then that all these things shall be dissolved, what manner of persons ought ye to be in all holy conversation and godliness,

12 Looking for and hasting unto the coming of the day of God, wherein the **heavens being on fire shall be dissolved,** and the elements shall melt with fervent heat?

13 Nevertheless we, according to his promise, look for new heavens and a new earth, wherein dwelleth righteousness.

When?

If you are a Bible believer you know that the U.S. is going to suffer the fire of God's wrath. But the question is *when*. If it burns after we are raptured out, we can console ourselves. But if we as a nation are destroyed before the Rapture, then our concern might be, "How much will it cost me to build an underground bunker and stock it with several months' worth of food and water?"

It goes back to the question of when the invasion by Magog and assisting nations takes place. If it is before the Rapture, as I tend to think, then expect judgment fire on the isles (U.S.) before we leave here. My best guess is that the Magog invasion takes place less than three years (could be more) before the Rapture, based on three things.

> If you are a Bible believer you know that the U.S. is going to suffer the fire of God's wrath. But the question is *when.*

1. The destruction of Magog's forces east of the Dead Sea is not the same event as the battle of Armageddon that takes place in the valley of Megiddo in northern Israel. And there is nothing in the book of Revelation that provides for the events described in Magog's invasion.

2. Antichrist gains power by his impressive ability to "make war" and bring peace to Israel (Revelation 13:7; Daniel 8:25). It would appear that the Megiddo battle must be over before the beginning of the reign of Antichrist. It is not until the three-and-one-half-year

mark that Antichrist reveals his dark side and God's judgment begins to be released upon the earth.

3. It will take seven years on top of seven months to "cleanse the land" after the destruction of Magog (Ezekiel 39:12, 16). In the latter part of the seven years, perhaps three and one-half years into the Tribulation, the Jews will come under persecution by Antichrist and be forced to flee for their lives. It would be unthinkable that they could—or would—continue to "cleanse the land" while the seal, trumpets, and vile judgments are taking place and men are hiding in the dens and rocks of the earth, praying that they will die to gain release from the plagues (Revelation 6:16). And the Jews come under lethal persecution if they fail to worship the beast (Revelation 13:15). There is just no way to confound Ezekiel's Magog judgment with the events of the Tribulation.

I don't think God intended for us to know precisely when the Magog invasion would occur. If we did, then the Rapture could not be imminent as we believe it is. If we knew it took place before the Rapture, we would not be looking for the blessed hope at any moment, but at Magog's military movements.

> I don't think God intended for us to know precisely when the Magog invasion would occur.

We do know that the fire is not going to completely annihilate any country, for when Jesus comes back at the end of the seven years, the nations will still be intact (Matthew 25:32), and even at the end of the Millennium (Revelation 21:24) and into eternity the nations will still maintain their integrity (Revelation 22:2).

Other Suggested Passages

JEREMIAH 50–51

There have been attempts to identify the U.S. with Jeremiah 50 and 51. In my less-learned days I also considered the plausibility of that interpretation. But a cursory reading clearly reveals that the text is about Babylon of old, not a figurative Babylon representing the U.S.

THE GREAT HARLOT

Others have attempted to read the U.S.—or even New York City and the financial markets—into Revelation 17. That is so far off base that it doesn't even need refuting. To come up with that interpretation you would have to treat the words of the Bible with a great deal of disrespect. Words matter.

BRITISH ISRAELISM

Then there are various groups, often associated with so-called Aryan supremacy, that have attempted to equate the Indo-Europeans, especially the British, with the so-called ten lost tribes, known as Israel. Again, that position has been so thoroughly refuted that it is like answering a fool to even address the subject.

Summation of the U.S. in Prophecy

It is American vanity to think the U.S. is so important that we must be the true Israel of God, or that we should play some leading role in the last days. God is focused on Israel as things wind down. He has begun the process that will lead to their being "grafted" back into the tree, and time marches to a clock located in Jerusalem. The U.S. is just a part of the Gentile nations. And we anticipate the near future when "the fullness of the Gentiles be come in" and "all Israel shall be saved" (Romans 11:24–26).

> It is American vanity to think the U.S. is so important that we must be the true Israel of God . . .

For I will gather all nations against Jerusalem to battle; and the city shall be taken, and the houses rifled, and the women ravished; and half of the city shall go forth into captivity, and the residue of the people shall not be cut off from the city. (**Zechariah 14:2**)

Therefore wait ye upon me, saith the LORD, until the day that I rise up to the prey: for my determination is to gather the nations, that I may assemble the kingdoms, to pour upon them mine indignation, even all my fierce anger: for all the earth shall be devoured with the fire of my jealousy. (**Zephaniah 3:8**)

I will also gather all nations, and will bring them down into the valley of Jehoshaphat, and will plead with them there for my people and for my heritage Israel, whom they have scattered among the nations, and parted my land. (**Joel 3:2**)

Objections to a Literal (Normal, Grammatical) Interpretation

The highly acclaimed Jamieson, Fausset, and Brown commentary written in 1871 lists six objections to a literal interpretation of the prophecy. His objections were based on the geopolitical conditions he observed in his day—always a mistake where the Word of God is concerned—and on the Preterist eschatological perspective descended from Rome. Blessed are ye who don't see and yet believe.

1. The **first reason** JF&B gives for not taking the prophecy literally is that it is "ideal" in nature, which is to say it is figurative and so can't be literal—a waste of paper and an affront to our intelligence.

2. The **second reason** is that, "The nations congregated are selected from places most distant from Israel, and from one another, and therefore most unlikely to act in concert (Persians and Libyans, etc.)." It is true that at the time the prophecy was given there were enemies of Israel that were much closer at hand and were an imminent threat, and the nations selected in the prophecy were never a threat to Israel and were well beyond the knowledge of most Israelites. Additional nations and peoples are mentioned as part of the invasion force, comprising most of the Western nations. So unless one just believed the words of God, it would have been difficult to understand why Ukraine, Great Britain, and Germany would invade the deserted land of Palestine in 600 BC or the late 1800s AD.

3. JF&B's **third reason** the prophecy could not be taken literally is that "the whole spoil of Israel could not have given a handful . . . to myriads of invaders," which was certainly true in the late 1800s. Only in my lifetime has that changed. Israel is now a tempting target.

4. Its **fourth reason** is that the stench of such a large number of dead would make life unbearable for the occupants of the land. But the Bible does observe that the slain lying upon the ground will "stop the noses of the passengers."

5. JF&B admits that the **fifth objection** to a literal interpretation is probably unfounded.

6. JF&B's **sixth objection** is that the passage is altogether too "carnal" to be associated with the second coming of Christ—too much death and destruction. Well, I think hell is too carnal. Who has a right to question God's morality?

When one passes judgment on the words of God because they don't measure up to current conditions or human reasoning, it is called unbelief.

When one passes judgment on the words of God because they don't measure up to current conditions or human reasoning, it is called unbelief.

When men who claim to believe the Bible find the words of God hard to believe, they have responded in one of two ways: to reduce it to poetry and parable, saying it is symbolic of some great principle, or to suggest that a distant-past historical event could have been the fulfillment. It is a lot easier to profess belief in past miracles than to go out on a limb proclaiming future miracles. This Preterism, the eschatological theological position of Roman Catholicism and Protestantism, was born of unbelief.

> Therefore wait ye upon me, saith the LORD, until the day that I rise up to the prey: for my determination is to **gather the nations,** that I may assemble the kingdoms, to pour upon them mine indignation, even all my fierce anger: for all the earth shall be devoured with the fire of my jealousy. (**Zephaniah 3:8**)

Shifting Interpretations

After having witnessed sixty years of prophecy teachers shifting their interpretations to match apparent current events, it is easy to disregard everyone who raises money or sustains their popularity by hovering over those current events and playing on the fears of apocalyptic watchers and the hopes of those who "love his appearing."

The interpretation of Bible prophecy is never based on geopolitical observation. A prophecy is the same in the tenth century as in the twenty-first. The shifting political climate has no bearing. If a Bible prophecy is in contradiction to realities on the ground, we can be sure the prophecy is correct and, in time, realities on the ground will change.

> The interpretation of Bible prophecy is never based on geopolitical observation.

However, having disparaged my fellow teachers, I am going to step into their shoes to observe current international trends that could be the prelude to the fulfillment of Ezekiel 38–39.

Interpreting the text itself, and disregarding any current events, we see a scenario that has much similarity to current events. This has never been the case in the past 2,700 years. Conditions are uniquely similar to the prelude to the Magog invasion. Consider the realities of the text and compare them to current events.

1. The land of Israel will have lain waste for many years.

2. Jews will have been scattered among the nations.

3. The nation itself will be "brought forth out of the nations."

4. "In the latter years, after many days," Jews "will be gathered out of many people" and reoccupy their ancient homeland.

5. The land will have been conquered by force—"brought back from the sword."

6. Israel will be "dwelling safely in the land."

7. Israel will be a "land of unwalled villages."

8. There will be a coalition of "many nations" from the "four quarters of the earth," headed by descendants of Japheth, come down to the region to settle another geopolitical disturbance.

9. They will be assisted by Turkey, Iran, Ethiopia, and Libya.

10. The invasion will "come like a storm" and be "like a cloud to cover the land."

11. The invasion will take place from the north down through Turkey, Lebanon, and Syria.

12. While there, they will "think an evil thought," realizing this would be a good opportunity to invade Israel.

13. Saudi Arabia and Yemen will not participate in the invasion but will question the intentions of the invasion.

14. And most glaringly, no mention is made of Israel's many enemies during the seventh century BC when the prophecy was made, the majority of which no longer exist.

In Your Face!

The question we must ask is, how likely is it that a coalition of united nations led by Western nations and assisted by Muslim nations including Iran and Libya should be in the Middle East with a display of force and suddenly decide to take the opportunity to conquer Israel?

Conclusion

If you wish to know more about Ezekiel 38–39, you will need to search your concordance for every time the different people groups or nations are mentioned. I found that much more helpful and accurate than historical studies and genetics. Be careful about taking the word of any one Bible dictionary, commentary, or commentator—including this author. There are a great deal of highly varied opinions. It is helpful to affirm one's interpretation with the weight of historical sources, but there is only one sure source—the Word of God. If you are an English reader, you will discover the words of God accurately preserved only in the King James Bible.

Ezekiel 38 (KJV)

1 And the word of the Lord came unto me, saying,

2 Son of man, set thy face against Gog, the land of Magog, the chief prince of Meshech and Tubal, and prophesy against him,

3 And say, Thus saith the Lord God; Behold, I am against thee, O Gog, the chief prince of Meshech and Tubal:

4 And I will turn thee back, and put hooks into thy jaws, and I will bring thee forth, and all thine army, horses and horsemen, all of them clothed with all sorts of armour, even a great company with bucklers and shields, all of them handling swords:

5 Persia, Ethiopia, and Libya with them; all of them with shield and helmet:

6 Gomer, and all his bands; the house of Togarmah of the north quarters, and all his bands: and many people with thee.

7 Be thou prepared, and prepare for thyself, thou, and all thy company that are assembled unto thee, and be thou a guard unto them.

8 After many days thou shalt be visited: in the latter years thou shalt come into the land that is brought back from the sword, and is gathered out of many people, against the mountains of Israel, which have been always waste: but it is brought forth out of the nations, and they shall dwell safely all of them.

9 Thou shalt ascend and come like a storm, thou shalt be like a cloud to cover the land, thou, and all thy bands, and many people with thee.

10 Thus saith the Lord God; It shall also come to pass, that at the same time shall things come into thy mind, and thou shalt think an evil thought:

11 And thou shalt say, I will go up to the land of unwalled villages; I will go to them that are at rest, that dwell safely, all of them dwelling without walls, and having neither bars nor gates,

12 To take a spoil, and to take a prey; to turn thine hand upon the desolate places that are now inhabited, and upon the people that are gathered out of the nations, which have gotten cattle and goods, that dwell in the midst of the land.

13 Sheba, and Dedan, and the merchants of Tarshish, with all the young lions thereof, shall say unto thee, Art thou come to take a spoil? hast thou gathered thy company to take a prey? to carry away silver and gold, to take away cattle and goods, to take a great spoil?

14 Therefore, son of man, prophesy and say unto Gog, Thus saith the Lord God; In that day when my people of Israel dwelleth safely, shalt thou not know it?

15 And thou shalt come from thy place out of the north parts, thou, and many people with thee, all of them riding upon horses, a great company, and a mighty army:

16 And thou shalt come up against my people of Israel, as a cloud to cover the land; it shall be in the latter days, and I will bring thee against my land, that the heathen may know me, when I shall be sanctified in thee, O Gog, before their eyes.

17 Thus saith the Lord God; Art thou he of whom I have spoken in old time by my servants the prophets of Israel, which prophesied in those days many years that I would bring thee against them?

18 And it shall come to pass at the same time when Gog shall come against the land of Israel, saith the Lord God, that my fury shall come up in my face.

19 For in my jealousy and in the fire of my wrath have I spoken, Surely in that day there shall be a great shaking in the land of Israel;

20 So that the fishes of the sea, and the fowls of the heaven, and the beasts of the field, and all creeping things that creep upon the earth, and all the men that are upon the face of the earth, shall shake at my presence, and the mountains shall be thrown down, and the steep places shall fall, and every wall shall fall to the ground.

21 And I will call for a sword against him throughout all my mountains, saith the Lord God: every man's sword shall be against his brother.

22 And I will plead against him with pestilence and with blood; and I will rain upon him, and upon his bands, and upon the many people that are with him, an overflowing rain, and great hailstones, fire, and brimstone.

23 Thus will I magnify myself, and sanctify myself; and I will be known in the eyes of many nations, and they shall know that I am the Lord.

Ezekiel 39

1 Therefore, thou son of man, prophesy against Gog, and say, Thus saith the Lord God; Behold, I am against thee, O Gog, the chief prince of Meshech and Tubal:

2 And I will turn thee back, and leave but the sixth part of thee, and will cause thee to come up from the north parts, and will bring thee upon the mountains of Israel:

3 And I will smite thy bow out of thy left hand, and will cause thine arrows to fall out of thy right hand.

4 Thou shalt fall upon the mountains of Israel, thou, and all thy bands, and the people that is with thee: I will give thee unto the ravenous birds of every sort, and to the beasts of the field to be devoured.

5 Thou shalt fall upon the open field: for I have spoken it, saith the Lord God.

6 And I will send a fire on Magog, and among them that dwell carelessly in the isles: and they shall know that I am the Lord.

7 So will I make my holy name known in the midst of my people Israel; and I will not let them pollute my holy name any more: and the heathen shall know that I am the Lord, the Holy One in Israel.

8 Behold, it is come, and it is done, saith the Lord God; this is the day whereof I have spoken.

9 And they that dwell in the cities of Israel shall go forth, and shall set on fire and burn the weapons, both the shields and the bucklers, the bows and the arrows, and the handstaves, and the spears, and they shall burn them with fire seven years:

10 So that they shall take no wood out of the field, neither cut down any out of the forests; for they shall burn the weapons with fire: and they shall spoil those

that spoiled them, and rob those that robbed them, saith the Lord God.

11 And it shall come to pass in that day, that I will give unto Gog a place there of graves in Israel, the valley of the passengers on the east of the sea: and it shall stop the noses of the passengers: and there shall they bury Gog and all his multitude: and they shall call it The valley of Hamongog.

12 And seven months shall the house of Israel be burying of them, that they may cleanse the land.

13 Yea, all the people of the land shall bury them; and it shall be to them a renown the day that I shall be glorified, saith the Lord God.

14 And they shall sever out men of continual employment, passing through the land to bury with the passengers those that remain upon the face of the earth, to cleanse it: after the end of seven months shall they search.

15 And the passengers that pass through the land, when any seeth a man's bone, then shall he set up a sign by it, till the buriers have buried it in the valley of Hamongog.

16 And also the name of the city shall be Hamonah. Thus shall they cleanse the land.

17 And, thou son of man, thus saith the Lord God; Speak unto every feathered fowl, and to every beast of the field, Assemble yourselves, and come; gather yourselves on every side to my sacrifice that I do sacrifice for you, even a great sacrifice upon the mountains of Israel, that ye may eat flesh, and drink blood.

18 Ye shall eat the flesh of the mighty, and drink the blood of the princes of the earth, of rams, of lambs, and of goats, of bullocks, all of them fatlings of Bashan.

19 And ye shall eat fat till ye be full, and drink blood till ye be drunken, of my sacrifice which I have sacrificed for you.

20 Thus ye shall be filled at my table with horses and chariots, with mighty men, and with all men of war, saith the Lord God.

21 And I will set my glory among the heathen, and all the heathen shall see my judgment that I have executed, and my hand that I have laid upon them.

22 So the house of Israel shall know that I am the Lord their God from that day and forward.

23 And the heathen shall know that the house of Israel went into captivity for their iniquity: because they trespassed against me, therefore hid I my face from them, and gave them into the hand of their enemies: so fell they all by the sword.

24 According to their uncleanness and according to their transgressions have I done unto them, and hid my face from them.

25 Therefore thus saith the Lord God; Now will I bring again the captivity of Jacob, and have mercy upon the whole house of Israel, and will be jealous for my holy name;

26 After that they have borne their shame, and all their trespasses whereby they have trespassed against me, when they dwelt safely in their land, and none made them afraid.

27 When I have brought them again from the people, and gathered them out of their enemies' lands, and am sanctified in them in the sight of many nations;

28 Then shall they know that I am the Lord their God, which caused them to be led into captivity among the heathen: but I have gathered them unto their own land, and have left none of them any more there.

29 Neither will I hide my face any more from them: for I have poured out my spirit upon the house of Israel, saith the Lord God.

On a Side Note...

Harry and Eddie:
The Friendship that Changed the World

The Odd Way God Made Sure Israel Became a Nation

There is an interesting piece of history found in the pages of a children's history book called *Harry and Eddie* by Beverly Joan Boulware.

The final fate of Israel ever becoming a nation was held in the hands of a very reluctant President Harry Truman. During the beginning of his presidency Truman had had some very rude Jewish leaders threaten him and put him under political pressure. It really irritated him, effectively shutting the door to them for any future favors. So when the time came for them to put an appeal before him concerning a possible homeland for the Jews coming out of the holocaust, the President would not even receive them. They enlisted the help of the famous Jewish biochemist Dr. Chaim Weizmann. Dr. Weizmann invented a process that was used to make ammunition for World War I weapons, and for that he was to be given a written promise by the British government (Balfour Declaration) that they would support the creation of a place for the Jews to settle in the ancient

Beverly Joan Boulware

Now available from No Greater Joy Ministries at ngj.org/harryeddie

land of Israel. The old man traveled across the sea in order to appeal to President Truman concerning Israel becoming a nation, but our president refused to even see the famous old man. All was lost until the leaders of the Jewish community remembered that when President Harry Truman was a boy his best friend was a Jewish boy named Eddie Jacobson. The boys had served together in World War I and when the war ended they had entered business together. For all those years they had been the closest of friends. Those that knew the President knew that he loved and trusted his old friend so they assumed that he would surely listen to him. They contacted Eddie and asked him to call the President and ask him to see the old biochemist, Dr. Weizmann. President Truman told his friend, Eddie that he would not see or have anything to do with the Jewish community as they had been so rude. Eddie could not take no for an answer. He knew that thousands of Jewish people had had their property stolen during the war. They had nowhere to go, no home, business, no money and their health was broken; these were a desperate people. They needed a place to call home. Eddie went to Washington DC to try to persuade the President to see the Dr. Weizmann. Of course, when Eddie Jacobson got to the capital building he was told that
no one saw the President
without an appointment.
While Eddie stood in the
hall trying to decide what
to do, he could hear his old
friend's loud commanding
voice. Eddie simply walked
toward the familiar voice.
For some strange reason,
no one stopped him; not
the guard, not the other
workers, and not even the
President's private secretary.
When the Harry Truman
looked up from working
at his desk there sat Eddie
waiting to be heard.

President Truman and Eddie Jacobson

President Truman was glad to see his friend but continued to steadfastly refuse to see Dr. Weizmann. Eddie persisted with good arguments until the President saw that this was of utmost important to his lifelong loyal friend, so he finally agreed to give Dr. Weizmann a chance to be heard. Once Truman heard Dr. Weizmann's reports

President Truman and Dr. Weizmann

of the desperate needs of the Jewish people, he saw that the honorable thing to do was fight for a Jewish homeland. President Truman knew it would take more votes so he began to call members of the United Nations asking them to stand with him in making Israel a nation. A few weeks later there was a vote which declared Israel a nation and gave a homeland to the Jewish people. Eleven minutes after the vote President Harry Truman put in a call to Israel's first Prime minister, making the United States the first country to contact the new government of Israel and give it diplomatic recognition.

It is amazing how tenuous the events were in making Israel a nation after over 1,000 years of being dispersed over the whole world. More amazing is the fact that the old Hebrew language, which had been basically lost, was also restored. The land that was useless came alive under the careful craftsmanship of the hard working Jewish folks. Soon there were schools, colleges, hospitals, and institutions of science, some of the finest in the world. In a very short few years the tiny nation became a military force to be reckoned with. In my lifetime, while the whole world watched, Israel was born, grew, and flourished. It was the bond, trust and respect that two young boys had for one another that opened the door.

GOOD AND EVIL

THE ULTIMATE COMIC BOOK ACTION BIBLE

God chose to introduce Himself to mankind, not through principles, concepts, or doctrine; but through stories of prophecy, war, mercy, judgment, miracles, death, life, and forgiveness.

Written by Michael Pearl and drawn by former Marvel comic artist Danny Bulanadi.

This is God's redemption plan told chronologically from Genesis to Revelation. Those familiar with the Marvel Comic book format greatly appreciate this classic, high-quality, full-color art.

Available in English, Spanish, Russian, Chinese, Ukrainian, Japanese, Hebrew and many other languages.

Also available as a professionally animated video series.

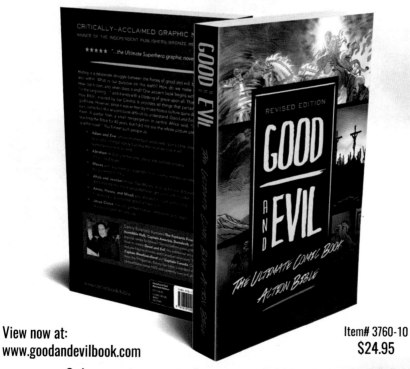

Michael Pearl's oil painting of Revelation

Huge Revelation Banner

The original painting has been reproduced on heavy duty vinyl, 35" high by 80" wide and can be used for personal or group Bible study, as well as in churches. Verses are marked beside the images on the painting. This is a great resource for pastors, chaplains and anyone who teaches bible studies, Sunday school or homeschool. Comes with 6 free handbooks/study guides, additional handbooks may be bought at $5.00 each. Made out of heavy duty vinyl, hemmed on all sides and reinforced with grommets. Comes with 6 free handbooks. Additional handbooks may be bought for $5.00 each. If you always thought the book of Revelation was a mystery and too hard to understand, now is your opportunity to approach it in a way that makes it easy to study.

Item# 8130-13

$89.95

52

Revelation Poster & Handbook

Michael Pearl's original nine-foot canvas painting, depicting the events described by John in the book of Revelation, has been reproduced on thick, 19" x 38" poster paper. Michael has prepared a handbook to go with the painting, which makes a great study guide for personal or group Bible study. Verses are marked beside the images on the painting, and the handbook gives additional references out of the Old an New Testaments. If you always thought the book of Revelation was a mystery and too hard to understand, now is your opportunity to approach it in a way that makes it easy to study. The poster ships in a protective hard cylinder.

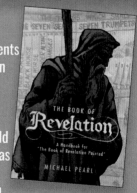

Item# 8130-10

$12.95

Order now at *nogreaterjoy.org* or call *866-292-9936*

Resource Catalog

For more material published by NGJ, including books and videos on child training, downloadable audio teachings on Bible topics, homeschooling resources and much more, visit our website at www.nogreaterjoy.org or call toll-free, 866-292-9936.

Volume discounts are available on many items. We also offer a Distributorship Program for churches and resellers. Call for more info.

50 Questions & 50 Answers

Unscripted and spontaneous, follow Mike around the farm as he answers your Bible questions. Varied questions and answers in a changing context makes this series captivating. DVD, 270 min.

Good and Evil

An award-winning graphic novel depicting the Bible stories from Genesis to Revelation, written by Michael Pearl and featuring spectacular full-color artwork by former Marvel Comic artist Danny Bulanadi. Available in full color in English, Spanish, Chinese and Russian. Many more languages available in black-and-white through Print-on-Demand. By Michael Pearl. 320 pages.

Now also available as an engaging Animated Series with 7+ hrs. of dramatized content in a 3-DVD Set, or as an Audio Book (MP3 CD).

By Divine Design

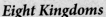

If you are philosophically minded, this book will appeal to you. It addresses the question, "Why, God, did you let this happen?" By Michael Pearl. 85 pages.

Eight Kingdoms

Understand the Bible by discovering the differences between the kingdom of God and the kingdom of Heaven. By Michael Pearl. 200 pages.

Bible Teaching Audio

Verse-by-Verse Audio Teaching

Michael Pearl teaches in-depth through the New Testament, examining each word and its usage. Practical and foundational Bible teaching that will build your faith in the Word of God and teach you to study on your own.

- Matthew (MP3 CD)
- Mark (MP3 CD)
- Luke (MP3 CD)
- John (MP3 CD)
- Acts (MP3 CD)
- Romans (MP3 CD)
- 1 Cor. & Colossians (MP3 CD)
- 2 Corinthians (MP3 CD)
- Galatians (MP3 CD)
- Ephesians (MP3 CD)
- Philippians (MP3 CD)
- 1 & 2 Thessalonians (MP3 CD)
- Hebrews (MP3 CD)
- James (MP3 CD)
- 1 & 2 Peter (MP3 CD)
- 1, 2, 3 John & Jude (MP3 CD)
- Verse-by-Verse Bible Teaching Audio Library (USB)

Bible Topics MP3s/CDs

Various topical studies taught by Michael Pearl from the King James Bible, of interest to new Christians as well as Bible scholars. This is some great in-depth material to grow the faith of believers! They also make great gifts.

- Two Steps to Heaven (Audio CD)
- 50 Sins (MP3 CD)
- ABC Bible Songs (Audio CD)
- Am I Saved? (MP3 CD)
- Body, Soul & Spirit (MP3 CD)
- Born Sinners, or Made Sinners? (Audio CD)
- Cherubim (Audio CD)
- Gospel to the Amish (MP3 CD)
- Prodigal Son (Audio CD)
- The Rich Man and Lazarus (Audio CD)
- Righteousness (MP3 CD)
- Sin No More & Sanctification (MP3 CD)
- Sinful Nature (MP3 CD)
- Sowing and Reaping (Audio CD)
- Witnesses Unto Me (MP3 CD)

Additional Bible Resources

- 1 John 1:9: The Protestant Confessional (Booklet, 23 pages)
- Baptism in Jesus' Name (Booklet, 17 pages)
- To Betroth or Not to Betroth (Booklet, 28 pages)
- The Gap Fact (Booklet, 30 pages)
- In Defense of Biblical Chastisement (Booklet, 29 pages)
- Justification and the Book of James (Booklet, 26 pages)

- Learning from the Atheists (Booklet, 32 pages)
- Pornography: Road to Hell (Booklet, 12 pages)
- Repentance (Book, 44 pages)
- Romans ch. 1-8 Commentary (Book, 222 pages)
- Who is the Antichrist? (Book, 96 pages)
- The Gap Fact and Out-Of-Whack Creation Scientism (Book,160 pages)

Science of Addiction and the Brain

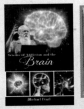

Addiction is the state of being enslaved to a substance or habit. At the 2014 Smoky Mountains Shindig, Michael delivered five packed messages supported by 185 animated PowerPoint™ slides on this subject. DVD, 222 min.

Revelation Poster/ Handbook

Print of Michael's original painting showing the events of Revelation in chronological order. The poster is 18"× 39" in. on heavy, glossy paper.

Also available as a large banner, 36" x 80". See page 50 for details.

Full product catalog available at **www.nogreaterjoy.org**

Made in the USA
Monee, IL
20 July 2024